Black Woman a Book of Poetry & Thoughts By

T.Stone

Copyright © 2020 T. Stone

All rights reserved.

Diverse Mediumz

ISBN: 9781732098947

DEDICATION

Dear black woman, you have to be loud in a world that have constantly tried to silence you!

Your blood is golden and your mind is magical. Keep tapping into your black girl magic and blessing the world with what it needs

- Tiana Nicole AKA T.Stone

CONTENTS

#1 2019

#2 King

#3 Revolution

#4 Love

#5 Knowledge of Blacks

#6 Message to my Son

#7 Numbers Never Lie

#8 Young Old School Black Love

#9 Signs of Nature

#10 Speechless

#11 Class Still in Session

#12 Manifesting my Destiny

#13 Color Blind 20/20 Vision

ACKNOWLEDGMENTS

Special recognition to the contributions of photography from Btac Production.

Thank you for giving me a different reason every day to tell you how dope you are!!

2019

This world we're living in crazy,
young sons and daughters getting shot by cops daily.

Against the law to have abortions
colonizers want our babies!

Used us hundreds of years as slaves
and now they say black people lazy.

But me,
I just know better because a cotton picker raised me.
I think about the 10 cents she said she got a week
every time they paid me.

Can't help but feel like the job system just some modern
day slavery.

Or is it the jail system?

I'm tryna tell sista,
so many traps in place just so you can fail sista.

Or should I say fall?

Yea they tryna get us all
` make America the biggest concentration camp and
build up a wall.

But then that don't work,
so they like ok let's keep trying.

White pigs back to work
and black kids keep dying.

And if we ain't getting shot down
then it's the food we're eating.

Maybe Monsanto is the snake
and grocery stores are truly Eden.

Cause at the eve of this moment
we're destroying our atoms

by partaking this bullshyt
throwing off our balance.

Shyd
I don't know rather to report it to the
FDA,
DEA,
or the CDC
cause they all in cahoots to the bullshit that they feeding me.

Hell, look at all the infrastructures that prosper off those eating meat.

Then double profit when they medicate them for growing old, diseased, and weak.

Man look,
like I said,
this world we living in crazy.

Young sons and daughters getting shot by cops daily,

but it's against the law to have abortions cause the colonizers want our babies.

Used us hundreds of years as slaves
and now they say black people lazy.

Damn.

And this was 2019!!

DAMN!

I'm just trying to meet the male version of me.
A handsome deep thinking king with the verbs of a "G".
Catch him flying to his paper like the birds to a tree.

Not on the scene he's busy manifesting and attracting his dreams,
but until I meet him I'm staying focused no joking no distractions and things.

I don't care if it's for fun
I don't care what it be,
cause one day soon Ima tell my son
look on the globe and pick one, hell you can even pick two,
traveling the world living life like we won a pick 3
or playing ball for one of these racist owners in the fucking big leagues.

I'm just so woke, so dope, with fucking big dreams, and I'm locked into this shit, ain't no stopping with this shit. Knaw ain't no escaping, I can't be complacent I am the example, I'm my son's motivation
and mark my words when I tell you I'm gonna make it.

And what better way than you next to me?
Building up our family, the youth, and our legacy.
Picture that.
You're actually listening now, and if in fact
that's the case,
let me just take the time to say
that I don't have the time of day,
for jiving and bullshit
knaw ain' got no time to play,
but better believe my game fit.
I'm trying to take over the world
on some pinky and the Brain shit.
I bring the iron,
and you just gotta bring fist
and together we go hard
with everything we brang it.

What's a queen without a king, without a king what's a queen?
But, until I meet you I'm staying focused no joking, no distractions and things,
never know
maybe close
the day that we meet.
Got me smiling in my head
- umm now that would be sweet.

" GO AGAINST NATURE,
BUT STILL LET IT TAKE ITS COURSE.
WHAT DOES THAT MEAN?
IT MEANS, NEVER JUST LET LIFE HAPPEN
EVERYTHING IS CAUSE AND EFFECT
AND LAWS AND NATURE
EVEN THINGS WE DON'T ACCEPT OR
ACKNOWLEDGE.
MAKE IT YOUR BUSINESS TO INTERVENE IN
YOUR OWN LIFE AS MUCH AS POSSIBLE.
EVEN THOUGH YOU ARE DEALT A HAND,
IT IS YOU THAT CHOOSE THE CARDS YOU
PLAY." T- STONE

Black Woman

Black Woman

"When you think your world is falling apart, know that it is falling in place"

REVOLUTION ✊🏽✊🏾

My grind can't stop til I complete this mission
so ain't no sense of complaining
draining good energy bitchin'.
We getting closer to the end
of what's soon to be the beginning
of a nation of enslavement of our Nubian children.
While we focused on the basics they moving in quicker.

It's a war on our people
we being jet eye mind tricked,
but half of ya'll sleep too.
You thought slavery ended?
Well here comes the sequel.

They replaced KKK masks
with a state badge
and they rags
are now beige, black, or deep blue.
Guilty if you black,
it's not a law, but a fact.
All we are to them
is just a grant and a tax.
They running state tags
and your license,
which I call a "state pass"
to see if they bad,
so they ass
can make cash
off locking you up when they see you.

Licensed to pull the trigger to delete you,
licensed to pull the trigger to delete truth.
run your name thru the scanners then release juice.
It's a price on our heads,
I'm Bama bred I got complete proof.

That's why my purpose is to speak truth,

and spit it to the people
in a way you can convey
to break away
off what oppressors teach you

and as God is my witness

my mission

I will see through......

-REVOLUTION

Black Woman

LOVE

I think one of the biggest things that makes love burn
is the realization that he was never yours,
instead,
it was just your turn.

And it's hard to wrap my head around that
when I thought in fact
it was you that I earned.

But my value surpasses that of any man

it was from you that I learned.

Ain't no easy lesson though,
cause night like this
when I miss your kiss
it's you that I yearn.

But one day you will see

I stayed true to my words.

I got trust issues and love issues that's just due to my first.

Somedays are better than others,

but that's just due to my hurt

- Love...

KNOWLEDGE OF BLACKS

Chemistry is defined 1: as the branch of science that deals with the identification of the substances of which matter is composed; Definition 2: the investigation of their properties and the ways in which they interact, combine, and change and the use of these processes to form new substances.

Now I know a lot of you are really confused and stuck with this,
hated math and chemistry in school
feeling like you
really sucked at this

pardon my language in advance because I might cuss a bit.
But chemistry is really black history.

The root word "Chem" derived from Egypt and the suffix "istry" really means "KNOWLEDGE OF"...,

You see?

But, by the time we're taught it in school it's like blasphemy.

White teachers would point to a slave in a book and say that was me.

They say when you seek for knowledge you take over the ship,
so if you want to find me I'm where the captains be.
Following nothing but intuition,
creating my own wave
no NO KAP in me.
Breaking generational curses there ain't no trappin' me.

Just gotta transform yourself like you know alchemy.
You ain't gotta have the "juice" or the "game", all
you need is a brain and once you use it,
it's the same as a map and key.

MESSAGE TO MY SON

We got full control of how
we react to the moment
but,
no control of the time
my
thinking mind now realize that,
my 7-year-old asking me questions, like mama....
if white lies are little,
then are big lies black?

I told my son No,

and said "If you are ever seeking to know the truth of any real life facts"
my fingers then pointed to his head and said
the "answers to the universe is in our "hats"
Its embedded in our brain like a real live tat.
We are a true source of all of being like a real live tap
and if we all just used our powers then black lives will not just "matter"
blacks will thrive once they get their real eyes back.
He can barely stand to my knees,
but still he agreed,
yet most people over 30
still haven't realized that.

NUMBERS NEVER LIE

There is Power in numbers which will never lie
the passing of each moment is encoded with numerical ties.

I see numbers everywhere and I wander why certain ones stick to me.
I say,
it's confirmation through alpha numerical conversations stating what's meant to be.

If there is no such thing of coincidences only patterns, then surely there's a message meant for me.

Do you believe in destiny or divine right?
A person is rich within self, not from wealth, currently currency still can't buy divine life.

I awake every morning at 4:00 am, with deep thoughts in mind.
It's my conscious telling me to move forward strong on my journey
and put the weak thoughts behind.

Yea that's your spirit nudging for your participation in your own life.

That's God telling you to take control,

swim in rivers and lakes of gold.
Yea this world is yours
it is your divine right.

Knaw I ain't no easy go-er',
nor am I a saint,
but every day I awake to a new day to get it right
its God I thank.

I got the world in my hands, leaving me with branded palms
But its the only way to get what I make of life cause there's no other way to make what matter come to grips with my thumbs.

.

♥♥

♥♥YOUNG OL' SCHOOL BLACK LOVE♥♥
♥♥

I want that young ol' school black love.
I was 12 when I found it.

Crazy how even then,
being just a kid

I knew,

that love.

Back when we talked for hours on the phone,
back when guys showed you they liked you,
they didn't act tough.

Back when the feeling was new,
but still somehow I knew
just how to back it up.

Ol fast Ass'...

Thought I was doing wrong back then,
but glad I did now that I back track.

They told me it was puppy love …

but I still haven't found a love purer and that's fat facts.

Yea, bring back that.

Ol' school black love.

Love like Ol' School hip-hop

and hood movies from the 90's.

Love like Aaliyah Rock the Boat

Denzel Washington Remember the Titans.

Old school love,

back when feelings was revealed in love letters, wasn't no hiding.

Love like playing hide-n-go seek,
I mean hide-n-go get it.

Man life was just so much simpler when we were children.

Simple like them blank CD's that got dubbed.

Simple like 10 grams for a dime.

Simple like that ol' school black love.

A love that now ain't so simple for me to find.

So moments when I miss it,
I start reminiscing, and slip back into the times.

I see Everybody on social media be having suggestions,

well here's mine...
While we bringing back all the old school movies

can we please bring back that ol' school black love?

Cause Another season of what we currently have cannot make it.

It's under-budgeted and overrated.

I need that old school,

got me excited to go to school so I can see oh dude
"You hang up first,
no you hang up first",
hang up,
then call back up.

Yea I'm yearning for a good episode of that black love.

That Ol' school,

music groups singing in the rain so smooth

yea that's that way back love.

Crazy how even as a kid,

I knew way back then,

that,

that's love.

Yea that's what I need.

That Cliff and Claire Huxtable,

Harriet and Carl Winslow,

George and Louise.

Yea that love.

That Ol' school so true, young black love.

That Love…

SIGNS OF NATURE 🌱

I intend to be so intertwined with nature's signs that I arise by the sounds of the rooster's crows.
Rather I'm in east Africa or up one of Houston's roads.

I be so empowered when I'm hearing our real truth be told.
Cause let me tell you my Negus life is bigger than the black and white picture that you've been showed.

Because of generational curses we're born into slavery,

and ain't no saving we,

till we

start un-disguising

and minimizing
all the lies that at youth we're sold.

You gotta completely forget what you've been told.

The secret is,
you will reach so many points of right instead of wrong if
you just use your soul.

Let spirit be your guide.

No need to wreck your brain stressing, all blessings have testings,
but I assure you can't get no greater sense of direction,
not even if you used a road.

Knaw Ain't no greater way of staying afloat from the bullshyt, not even if you kneeled at the pool pit, or used a boat.

Can't no words replace the power of authentic truth, not even them SCRIPTured words that you...
use the most.

It doesn't matter the despair. When you spitting real shyt you broadcast seeds that will grow to produce the hope. So that makes you just as important as the preacher that prayed for you, or the neighborhood plug you paid to, package and produce the dope.

If you working on goals keep going your hardest and just know that you is' close.

Remember you a filthy rich nigga even if it don't get no bigger, because you can have money in the bank, but if you don't think thoughts of value... Well you is' broke.

If I was a celebrity and if it was in my hands, I wouldn't want fans, instead I would want you to revolt.
I'd stay one deep, with little to no peeps, because they be,

too hard to deal with.

And I get so frustrated with people,
because I have no understanding as to why for real shyt,
they bullshyt
and for bullshyt,
they...

do the most.

SPEECHLESS

My poetry be ...
Slow notioning,
Knaw let me rephrase myself,
I mean slow motioning

A body of words

that roll verbs
like the waves of the ocean seas.

Yeah I see you noticing,

my poetry, sweet poetry.

Can you for one moment, let my words pull you close to me?

SUN of God
you leave an imprint when your eyes kiss my skin,
I feel your stares so openly.

Slowly ... so slowly....

You hearing my rhymes so to speak.

Silently your eyes wording me
a sweet melody or a mental chime

telling me that it is time

Black Woman

you like to hear me scream yo' name
I like it when you dick me dine'.

I'm your personal Miss Nasty so to speak,
only for you I'll show the freak.
You'll be nodding your head to the beat of my drum like you composed a beat.

It is much more fun when you flow with me.

And when you catch my drift I'll give you more of me.

More of my
poetry,
sweet, poetry.

"Move away from both the automatic and cruise control mindset and instead steer toward cultivating a "stick- shift" mentality." -Tiana Nicole

CLASS STILL IN SESSION

Life is a journey
better yet let's say a school,
and knowledge is a weapon
better yet
let's say a tool.
So I play teacher's pet to the universe
and let the rest just play the fool.

Class is still in session and life steady submitting grades,
but my report card got A's
because I've acquired many lessons
and passed many tests.
Even when it required redo's I swear I did my best.

I gotta give this shyt my all, because I know nothing less.
All I know is I want more;

all I know is its divine.
I'm created for something special
and all I know is its time.

I can't put it no other way
all I know is this rhyme.
This world is up for grabs
and all I know is its mine.
But I can't conquer it alone,
Yet, I've seen so many who've tried.

I'm calling on the community
it's time we build as a team;
it seems
its better with unity.

You will be amazed at how much the world can change

if proper changes are made just within you and me.

Close your eyes and visualize,
it's so much harder than it seems,

that's how I know it can happen
if you can see.

Cause the mind is your servant
better yet
let's say your tool
and life is your journey
better yet
let's say your school.

The world is our classroom
created to be outgrown.

You have the right to question my words,
but there's no need to doubt long.

Instead live life with a purpose to progress and be all that
the world needs

there's no child left behind
one day we will all pass,
rather you don't or you do succeed.

But on the day you cross that stage,
instead of a graduation speech
it's a eulogy.

Even though it's not for you to read.

It is you who holds the power to write your life story
and that's the honest to God truth,
rather you don't or you do believe.

MANIFESTING MY DESTINY

Sometimes, I feel like I got entities after me
wanting me to fail,
but I will prevail.
It is my mission to master me.

God has blessed me with the master keys
so I must open up the doors for the generations after me.

So I'm designing,
constructing,
and upgrading my legacy.
I couldn't even tell you what this world is about,
but I vow to give this life the best of me,
manifest my destiny.
I don't believe in rest in peace,
the day I close my eyes for good,
will be the day I meet the rest of me.

I think death is when God will be testing me.

Shonuff life provided the lessons.
And Every time I put in the work.
Shonuff I'm provided blessings,
and I'm provided tools.
I've possessed them for some time,
but most I'm just beginning to use.
You see,
my memories were my own worst enemies.

I had to let go of the past
and focus more on the inner me.
I started mending myself,
and getting in- tuned spiritually.
I'm still making self-adjustments,
but now I do shyt differently.
I learned you must command it out the universe,
So ain't no more "pretty please".

Now I speak with authority,
like
"Give me that and give me these!"
Telling no asking...
I then move as if I know it has happened.
And every single time no lie, God rid my lack and meet
my needs.

"We get 86,400 seconds in a day, don't waste a damn second"- Tiana Nicole

COLOR BLIND/ 2020 VISION

Let's discuss colors when we're exploring our fashion.
because your outer appearance is just a border line fraction.
Life is about character and how we forward our actions.
Climaxes are created when we move forward on our passions.

If you're over 30 stop asking!

You don't need permission to be great,
and that goes for any age.

I was trained to fit in, but I rebelled,
and chose to renegade.

Cause I am a creator,
I am a producer,
I am nothing like you are ordinarily use to.
I understand this system will turn you out and use you.
Have you accomplishing someone else's goals
losing sight on what you were produced to do.

The "right" way of the world as we're taught is so wrong
til it's baffling!
We're exposed to modes that change our genetic codes
drastically.
Like why do we have all these reality shows that expose
no true reality?

We connect with the world through rusted coppers and
severed ties,
transmitting digitally projected actions with dialogues
consisting of cussing,
fussing,
and telling several lies.

(RIP)Gil Scott Heron

the Revolution is still not televised.

But hey

even the preacher and the teacher are paid and trained to tell us lies.
So we know damn well if TV broadcasted it they'll just be,
T-E-L-E-L-I-E-S, tele-lies!
But don't get me wrong so much you can learn, if you study the art of how to critically discern.

I love the power of movies because it gives us an opportunity to tell our side.

The Matrix portrayed this best,
this dimension is just,
a projected reality
of what we tell our eyes.

The brain is not capable of separating actuality
from the faulty reality
of what we tell our minds.

Black Woman

After the power loss of slaves, they changed up their tactics,
for years they attacked us
in fears of losing their stature.
They knew who we were before and even after

we were whitewashed,
but my mind is unshackled
and third eye open,
my subconscious is fully activated
and I get truly aggravated
as I watch how they got us distracted
by the disillusions of white, brown, and blackness.
It's time we wake up and realize

it's less about race
and more about the maintaining of order and classes.
dividing to conquer is how they're destroying our asses.

We are a democracy,
yet let representatives go to the capitol lobbying
for laws that grow businesses, but destroy citizens.

And these laws without our knowledge, they employ on
us without asking.

Fuck what you're use to, it's a war on our future.

Knaw we have no time to be distracted
especially with all this access.

Knaw it is no longer acceptable to not know. We no
longer can have voting polls up
and Blacks not go!
We can no longer go through a day,
week,
month,
or year and not grow!

We no longer can just tell our kids about what's right
and not show!
We are all we got
and they are killing us one by one.

We were born Kings and Queens ruling this land,
so the "man" Ain't hating on us just for fun.

really I don't believe in superiority

but instead evil people with powers who don't give a damn,

I say the "man" just for fun.

But just imagine what the world would be like...

If blacks once again ruled the lands under the sun.
It is amazing how much the black man has done.
I couldn't figure out what and why it felt wrong, til I looked deep within
Like "Oh it was a reason why in school I wasn't getting this"
it was because they started the history lessons showing slain slaves,
hung from ropes
bodies bonded by chains
and
other explicit images

Told us Columbus discovered America,
and if you get it wrong I'm failing ya
then issued a test.

it was all part of a plot
Insane how they rewrote our history

and not just a little piece they switched the setting
switched the time hell switched the whole damn plot

crazy how much destruction and deceit we reaped
just so they can keep
the whole damn lot.
Til' this day school encounters are the reason I can't trust
people no matter how nice they seem.

Forget the body,
you get the mind you got em' both

So
The images of slaves physically shackled was a tactic we
were psychologically attacked
as teens
So many attempts like got milk campaigns to rot and stiff

our brains and
calcify us mentally...

SO much thought goes into a scene so everything shown
was meant to be.
First we lost control of what they know
then we lost control of what they see.

now we got a world
filled with young misguided girls

and black boys with lost identities

being taught distorted history.

That's why It's so important that we step into our talents.

Having more black herbal doctors,
lawyers,
entrepreneurs,
and artists
will help in our balance.

Time to remove the blockage

Let's get back to
passing down knowledge,
help kids find themselves as young as possible
it's a disservice to wait until college.

It's time we get back to teaching our kids,
in fact, it's time we get back to teaching ourselves.
Our off springs only model what they see,

so get exposed to arts and traveling,
things that will compel our lives.

40 years later and the revolution is still un-televised.

It's our responsibility!
School and tube won't do it

We see it's up to us to restore our history.

Or the alternative is doing nothing
and just let the world destroy the potential of who our

kids were sent here to be.
But we know the outcome of what happens when you
don't know your past,
the inevitability of that
is that it will REPEAT!

Journal Excerpt of Tiana Nicole....

I've come to discover that more than often the problem is not that people don't understand you, the problem is that they do.

Their understanding of you forces them to vibrate higher when in your vicinity, sadly most choose and prefer to stay where they are.

In fact, it can be an uncomfortable feeling to experience something at the expense of a peer, had you been older, unattractive, handicapped or from another race or culture it can be "tolerated" and accepted, low vibrational people are uncomfortable seeing the growth from those they are similar or equivalent to i.e. same age, same gender, co-worker, classmate, neighbor, friend, peer, enemy.

It forces them to see what they lack, to become aware of their inabilities. Your surety reminds them of their uncertainty. Your happiness reminds them of their anger or sadness. Your hope is a reminder of their blank thoughts. Your energy is a reminder that life goes on and will get better.

It forces them to see that there is more to life. But low vibrating people do not care for that, it makes them uncomfortable. Rather you're' that person soaring or the one that is sore, my message to you is to keep vibrating high there is no end point to ascension. -T. Stone

An Actual Message to a friend from T. Stone

It is truly a journey and a process.
It's like you know what you want,
what you see for yourself,
the person you really are,
even if you're nowhere near it at the present moment,
even if no one understands or believe in your vision.
Sometimes it's not that people don't believe you are
destined for something
it's that they have their own idea of who you are or what
they want from you.
People will even give up on you altogether.
What the mass don't understand is rebirthing yourself is a
much more longer and painful process from when we
were originally birthed by our queen mothers.
Don't stop believing in yourself
or working toward your manifested destiny.
Your goal is bigger than a dream
it is your true reality
and you are put here to serve your purpose. - T- Stone

Black Woman

About the Author

T. Stone is more than an author; she is a visionary! Stone dubs herself as a creative mastermind. She has a B.A in Radio Television and Film and a M.A in Professional Communication, she is currently an 11th grade AP English Lang Teacher. Writing has been her outlet of expression since the age of 9. Curator of If I Was Yo' Daddy and If I Was Yo' Mama, I introduce poet, curator, and educator... T. Stone AKA Tiana Nicole.

Black Woman
a
Book of Poetry and Thoughts
Authored By
T.Stone

Published By
 Diverse Mediumz

www.ingramcontent.com/pod-product-compliance
Lightning Source LLC
Chambersburg PA
CBHW042328150426
43193CB00001B/15